W9-BSH-420

Ten-
Minute
Bento

VERTICAL.

Just cook up some rice, add a topping and your Ten-Minute Bento is done!

Since my daughters are going through a growth spurt, they want rice all the time, so bento boxes became a go-to menu option. Just one side dish doesn't seem skimpy if it's placed on rice. Plus it's easy to put together—if you've got ten minutes, you can make a bento. I'd even recommend this bento-making style to people who've never made one before in their lives.

—Megumi Fujii

✚ You only need one or two toppings

As long as you've got a decent bed of rice, don't worry if you're only adding one or two toppings—it'll still look and be filling. All you need is a main topping, some veggies for garnish and maybe some pickles, and you're good to go.

✚ It's easy to throw together!

Since everything is layered on top of the rice, you don't need to worry about different little containers jostling around. This is the speediest bento prep out there.

✚ Rice is nice!

I've chosen toppings that go well with rice, making the rice even tastier.

Note:
In this book, 1 Tbsp = 15 ml; 1 tsp = 5 ml; 1 C = 250 ml.
Microwave times are according to a 500w microwave. Each
microwave is different, so please keep an eye on foods as
they cook and adjust accordingly.

Mushroom-Stuffed Hamburger

Ham, Egg and Veggie Medley

Yuan-Style Salmon

Stir-Fry Namul

6

Delicious Standard Toppings

These toppings are stand-bys that I often use in bentos.
Just pop them on top of rice for a fresh take on staple recipes.
All you need are a couple of sides for an easy bento lunch.

Sliced Beef

Chicken Teriyaki

Sliced Pork Cutlet

Mushroom-Stuffed Hamburger Bento

These burgers are stuffed full of mushrooms, so they're filling but healthier.

Coated with rich sauce, this will make that rice vanish in no time!

8

Try making mini
fried eggs
using quail eggs!

Mushroom-Stuffed Hamburger

Serves 1
3 oz (80 g) ground beef and pork mix
A ┌ 1/2 bag enoki mushrooms, chopped
  │ 1 fresh shiitake mushroom, minced
  │ 2 quail eggs
  │ 2 Tbsp panko breadcrumbs
  │ 1/6 onion, grated
  └ Dash each salt, pepper
B ┌ 1 Tbsp each ketchup, Worcestershire sauce
  └ 1/2 Tbsp white wine
Vegetable oil

1. In a bowl, combine ground meat and mixture A and knead together. Divide into thirds and shape into patties.
2. Heat 1 tsp oil in a frying pan and cook patties over high heat for 30 seconds, then turn heat to low and cook for 3 minutes. Flip patties and repeat.
3. Add mixture B and bring to a boil, thoroughly coating burgers in the sauce.

Mini Sunny-Side Up Eggs

Serves 1
2 quail eggs
Lettuce, vegetable oil, salt and pepper, to taste

Heat 1/2 tsp oil in a frying pan over medium heat. Add quail eggs and fry sunny-side up. Season with salt and pepper. Garnish with lettuce.

Arrange:
Add cooked rice to bento box. Top with hamburgers, fried eggs and lettuce.

Finely chop the mushrooms so they blend well with the meat. Use any mushrooms you like.

Sliced Beef Bento

Sweet and salty beef is super appetizing and always a hit as a bento.
Add your favorite pickles as a palate-cleanser.

Add green peas for a pop of color and some extra nutrition!

This is a one-pan recipe!

Sweet and Salty Beef

Serves 1
3 oz (80 g) beef, thinly sliced
1/4 onion, thinly sliced
3 Tbsp frozen green peas
A ⎡ 2 Tbsp sake (or white wine)
⎢ 1 1/2 Tbsp soy sauce
⎢ 1 Tbsp mirin
⎣ 1/2 Tbsp sugar
Pickles, to taste
Vegetable oil

1. Heat 1/2 tsp oil in a frying pan over medium heat. Quickly stir-fry beef. Add onions and mixture A and bring to a boil. Add green peas and stir to coat.

Arrange:
Add cooked rice to bento box. Add sweet and salty beef and garnish with pickles.

If you stir well so the sauce has mostly coated the beef, there's less risk of the bento leaking.

Simple Bibimbap Bento

Just stir-fry ground meat and veggies on a busy morning!

Sweet and spicy, with a fragrance of sesame and loads of veggies!

Just stir-fry the meat and veggies together!

Stir-Fry Namul

Serves 1
3 oz (80 g) ground beef
1 3/4 oz (50 g) bean sprouts
1/4 carrot
5 snow peas
1/5 oz (5 g) Chinese cellophane noodles
A ⌈ 1 Tbsp soy sauce
  │ 1/2 Tbsp each sake, sugar, sesame oil
  │ 2" (5 cm) scallions, minced
  │ Pinch each grated ginger, garlic
  │ 1 tsp sesame paste
  └ Dash chili powder

1. Julienne carrot and snow peas. Rehydrate cellophane noodles in hot water, drain, then slice into bite-sized lengths. Knead mixture A into beef.
2. Heat beef in frying pan. Add all vegetables to the pan once the beef begins to release juice and stir-fry. Once the meat is thoroughly cooked and crumbly, add noodles and stir to soak up sauce.

Flattened Fried Egg

Serves 1
1 egg
Sesame oil, salt and pepper

Heat 1 tsp sesame oil in a frying pan over medium heat. Add egg. Break yolk and cook on both sides. Season with salt and pepper. Cut into bite-sized peices.

Arrange:
Add cooked rice to a bento box. Add namul and fried egg.

Breaking the egg yolk and frying well helps keep it unspoiled and adds a dash of color to the bento.

Quick Veggie Sides

These are easy to make in a pinch during busy mornings.
Add these to your standard toppings.

Just mix *tsukudani* kelp
with broccoli and pop into
the microwave.

Broccoli and Kelp

Serves 1 to 2
4 to 5 broccoli heads (1 3/4 oz)
A ⌐ 1 tsp *tsukudani* kelp (see
     appendix)
  └ 1/2 tsp water
1/2 tsp white sesame seeds

Combine broccoli and mixture A in
a heat-safe bowl, cover with plastic film and microwave for about 1
minute. Unwrap and sprinkle with
sesame seeds.

Butter is the secret ingredient.
This dish is also colorful.

Carrots with *Tarako*

Serves 1 to 2
1/2 small carrot
1/4 sac *tarako* (cod roe)
A ⌐ 1 tsp sake
     1/3 tsp butter
  └ 3 Tbsp water
Black pepper

1. Julienne carrot. Remove tarako
from membrane.
2. Add carrot, tarako and mixture
A to a frying pan and stir-fry over
medium heat until liquid is cooked
off. Add pepper to taste.

Rich miso flavor and
a toothsome texture

Miso Eggplant with Green Beans

Serves 1 to 2
1 small (Japanese or Italian) eggplant
3 green beans
A 2 tsp each miso, sake and sugar
Vegetable oil

1. Cut stem off of eggplants and slice
into 1/2" rings. Slice green beans on
the bias into 1 1/2" lengths. Combine
mixture A.
2. Heat 1 Tbsp oil in a frying pan
and sauté eggplant thoroughly over
medium heat. Add green beans and
mixture A and sauté.

Add *jako* for an added layer of deliciousness

Flash-Cooked Green Peppers

Serves 1 to 2
1 green bell pepper
1 Tbsp dried baby sardines (*chirimen jako*)
A ⌈ 1 Tbsp each sake, water
⌊ 1 tsp each soy sauce, mirin

1. Remove stem and seeds from bell pepper and thinly slice.
2. Add bell pepper, baby sardines and mixture A to a pan. Turn heat to medium and stir-fry until liquid is cooked off.

A sweet-and-salty side dish with fragrant scallions

Stir-fried Kabocha

Serves 1 to 2
1/10 kabocha (or other summer squash)
2" (5 cm) scallion
A ⌈ 1 tsp soy sauce
⌊ 1/2 tsp each sugar, sake
Vegetable oil

1. Remove stem and seeds from kabocha and slice into 1/4" thick bite-size wedges. Finely chop scallion.
2. Heat 1 tsp oil in a frying pan and sauté scallions over medium heat. Once scallions are fragrant, add kabocha and sauté. When the kabocha are mostly cooked through, add mixture A and stir.

A speedy microwave recipe. Sesame oil and salt add a Korean flair

Spicy Cabbage

Serves 1 to 2
2 leaves cabbage (3 1/2 oz)
A ⌈ 1 tsp sesame oil
⌈ Dash each salt, chili powder
⌊ 1 tsp white sesame paste

Shred cabbage into bite-size pieces and wrap in plastic. Microwave for 1 minute 30 seconds. Squeeze to drain. Dress with mixture A.

The salty-sweet sauce soaks into the rice for a delicious treat!

Chicken Teriyaki Bento

To streamline the process, make the vegetable side dish first, then the chicken teriyaki in the same frying pan.

Add nori to the rice!

Chicken Teriyaki

Serves 1
1/3 chicken thigh
2 tsp each soy sauce, sake
1 tsp sugar
Vegetable oil

1. Slice chicken into bite-size pieces on the bias. Sprinkle with soy sauce and sake.
2. Heat 1 tsp oil in a frying pan and cook each side of the chicken for 4 to 5 minutes over medium heat until well done. Dust with 1 tsp sugar and stir to coat until liquid has cooked off.

Sautéed Bell Peppers and Leeks

Serves 1
1 green bell pepper
1/4 leek (white part)
Vegetable oil, salt and pepper

1. Remove stem and seeds from bell pepper and julienne. Slice leek into 1 1/2" lengths.
2. Heat 1 tsp oil in a frying pan over medium heat and add leeks and peppers. Occasionally rotate leeks to evenly brown the sides. Sauté peppers. Season with salt and pepper.

Arrange:
Add cooked rice to a bento box and layer with grilled shredded nori. Add chicken teriyaki, bell peppers and leeks.

Adding sugar creates a delicious sheen.

Try breaking open the egg yolk and mixing it with the rice!

fourchette 2

Ham, Egg and Veggie Medley Bento

A super easy bento with things you'd always have on hand—eggs, ham and mixed vegetables.

Mixed vegetables and eggs whip up into a quick and easy bento!

Ham, Egg and Veggie Medley

Serves 1
1 egg
3 slices ham
4 Tbsp mixed vegetables (frozen)
Vegetable oil, salt, pepper

1. Slice ham in half, then into 1/2" pieces. Add mixed vegetables to a heat-safe dish and microwave, covered, for 40 seconds.
2. Heat 2 tsp oil in a frying pan over medium heat and add mixed vegetables in a donut shape. Layer ham inside the "donut hole" and add egg to the center. Cover with a lid and cook through. Season with salt and pepper.

Arrange:
Add cooked rice to a bento box and layer ham, egg and veggie medley on top. Add soy sauce or other seasoning to taste.

Covering with a lid after adding the egg ensures thorough cooking.

The fragrance of citrus whets your appetite!

Yuan-Style Salmon Bento

Pair citrusy salmon and spinach mixed with dried bonito for a very Japanese bento.

A frying pan is all you need, even with the fish topping!

Yuan-Style Salmon

Serves 1
1 fllet salmon
A ┌ 1 tsp soy sauce
   │ 1/3 tsp each sake, mirin
   └ 1 slice lemon (or yuzu)
Vegetable oil

1. Slice salmon into 3 or 4 pieces on the bias. Coat with mixture A and let marinate for at least 10 minutes.
2. Heat a small amount of oil in a frying pan over medium heat. Add salmon. Baste with marinade and cook each side 3 to 4 minutes. (You can also try grilling the salmon.)

Spinach with Bonito Flakes

Serves 1
3 handfuls of spinach
1 Tbsp dried bonito flakes (*katsuo*)
Soy sauce

1. Boil spinach, then drain. Squeeze out moisture and slice into 1 1/2-2" pieces.
2. Add 1/2 tsp soy sauce, mix, then squeeze out moisture. Add another 1/2 tsp soy sauce and dried bonito flakes and stir to mix.

Arrange:
Add cooked rice to a bento box. Add white sesame seeds. Add salmon and spinach. Garnish salmon with lemon (or yuzu) peel.

Marinate the salmon overnight so all you need to do in the morning is cook it.

Sliced Pork Cutlet Bento

These pork cutlets use thinly-sliced layers for a fluffy texture.
Garnish with plenty of cabbage.

Sauce-soaked
cutlets with rice is
irresistible!

Add dried plum rice seasoning to balance the flavors!

Sliced Pork Cutlets

Serves 1

3 oz (80 g) thinly sliced pork loin
Flour, whisked egg and panko breadcrumbs, as
 needed
Salt, pepper, frying oil and tonkatsu sauce, as
 needed

1. Layer slices of pork together. Season with salt
and pepper, dust with flour, baste with egg and
coat with breadcrumbs.
2. Heat frying oil until at medium frying
temperature and add pork cutlet. Flip, cooking
each side for 3 to 4 minutes or until well done.
Remove and drain oil. Slice into bite-size pieces.

Shredded Cabbage

Serves 1

2 leaves cabbage

Layer cabbage leaves and finely slice. Soak in
water to crisp. Drain well.

Arrange:

Add cooked rice to bento box and sprinkle dried
plum seasoning (*yukari*) if desired. Add cabbage
and layer pork cutlet on top. Garnish with your
favorite pickles. Dress with sauce as desired.

Using layered sliced pork
creates a light texture
that's eminently eatable.

Pasta and Bread Bentos:
Just Mix 'em Up Like Salads!

Using pasta or bread in place of rice makes for very light bentos.
Make them as you would a salad, mixing up with veggies and dressings.

2

Saifun Salad Bento

Saifun, or cellophane noodles, can be quickly reconstituted with hot water, making them perfect for use in fast bento-making.

The dressing is tangy and spicy with chili and lemon juice!

Use nam pla in the dressing!

Saifun Salad

Serves 1
1 1/2 oz (40 g) saifun (Chinese cellophane noodles)

Nam Pla Dressing:
1 Tbsp each nam pla (Thai fish sauce), lemon juice
1/2 Tbsp vegetable oil
1/2 tsp sugar
1 small red chili
Grated garlic, to taste

1. Soak cellophane noodles in hot water to soften, then drain well.
2. Combine Nam Pla Dressing ingredients. Add 1 Tbsp dressing to noodles and mix.

Salad Toppings

Serves 1
1/4 red onion
1/3 cucumber
3 oz (80 g) cooked shrimp
2 Tbsp peanuts

Slice onions and soak in water, then drain. Slice cucumber in half lengthwise, deseed, then slice thinly on the bias. Coat shrimp with some of the Nam Pla dressing. Roughly chop peanuts.

Arrange:
Add saifun salad to bento box. Add salad toppings in a colorful, neat arrangement. Pour remainder of dressing into a separate container to dress salad before eating.

Place saifun in a bowl and add hot water. Try cutting into bite-size pieces.

Add daikon and *hijiki* seaweed for a healthy boost!

Soba and Daikon Salad Bento

Boiling the sliced daikon and *hijiki* with the soba noodles will keep the noodles from sticking together when they cool.

Use wasabi mayo sauce!

Soba and Daikon Salad

Serves 1
1/2 serving soba noodles
2" (5 cm) daikon radish
1 Tbsp (5 g) *hijiki* seaweed (dried)
Wasabi Mayo Sauce:
⌈ 3 Tbsp mentsuyu (see appendix)
| 1 Tbsp mayonnaise
⌊ 1 tsp wasabi
Soy sauce

1. Julienne daikon. Soak hijiki in water to reconstitute.
2. Bring plenty of water to a boil. Add soba, daikon, hijiki and cook until soba is done (according to time listed on package).
3. Remove soba and vegetables from pot, rinse and drain well. Stir in 1 tsp soy sauce. Combine Wasabi Mayo Sauce ingredients.

Pork and Veggies

Serves 1
3 oz (80 g) thinly sliced pork loin
6 snow peas
1/2 C alfalfa sprouts

Bring plenty of water to a boil. Add pork and boil until browned. Strain, removing any emulsified fat. Blanch snow peas until they turn bright green. Drain. Rinse sprouts and squeeze out any water.

Arrange:
Add soba to bento box. Add pork, snow peas and sprouts. Sprinkle with black sesame seeds. Pour wasabi mayo sauce into a separate container to add to soba before eating.

Go ahead and boil the daikon and hijiki right along with the soba noodles. Add soy sauce once the soba is cooked and drained.

Pasta with Tuna and Broccoli Bento

Broccoli acts like pesto sauce for the pasta.
Short fusilli pasta works best for this dish.

The tuna makes this a very satisfying meal!

Add a squeeze of lemon!

Pasta with Tuna and Broccoli

Serves 1
1/2 small head broccoli
3 oz (80 g) fusilli pasta
1 small can tuna
1 red chili pepper
Dash minced garlic
Lemon, to taste
Salt, pepper, olive oil

1. Roughly chop broccoli. Add 1 qt water and 2 tsp salt to a pot and bring to a boil. Add pasta and broccoli and cook until pasta is done (according to time indicated on package).
2. Heat 1 1/2 Tbsp oil in a frying pan over low heat. Add garlic and sauté until lightly browned. Add chili pepper, drained tuna and pasta and sauté together.

Arrange:
Add pasta with tuna and broccoli to bento box. Top with a squeeze of fresh lemon.

Boil the broccoli with the pasta. Soft, crumbly broccoli blends well with the pasta.

Plain soy sauce goes great with vegetables!

Ramen Salad Bento

Use colorful vegetables for a salad-style arrangement.
Add oil to the noodles to keep them from sticking together when cooled.

Soy sesame dressing is perfect for this dish!

Ramen

Serves 1
1 serving ramen
Soy Sesame Dressing:
- 1 Tbsp soy sauce
- 1/2 Tbsp vinegar
- 1 tsp wholegrain mustard
- 1/2 tsp each sugar, sesame oil

Sesame oil

1. Bring plenty of water to a boil. Add ramen and cook (according to time indicated by package directions). Strain, rinse and drain well. Mix with 1 tsp sesame oil.
2. Combine ingredients for Soy Sesame Dressing.

Ramen Salad Toppings

Serves 1
5 green beans
2 leaves lettuce
2 slices ham
1 egg
Salt, pepper, vegetable oil

1. Chop green beans into 1 1/2" pieces. Boil with ramen. Drain. Shred lettuce into bite-size pieces. Slice ham into thin strips.
2. Whisk egg and add a dash each of salt and pepper. Heat 1 tsp oil in a frying pan and cook egg over medium heat, stirring constantly until crumbled.

Arrange:
Add ramen to bento box. Add vegetables, ham and crumbled egg. Pour soy sesame dressing into a separate container to add to ramen salad before eating.

Adding sesame oil to boiled ramen noodles adds a wonderful flavor.

Freezable Mini Desserts

If you make a batch of desserts when you have spare time and put them in the freezer to keep, you can add something sweet to bento lunches in a snap.
Add it to the lunch box still frozen, and it'll thaw by lunchtime!

Slice these into easy-to-eat strips
Brownies

Yields one 8" x 8" pan
1/2 C (100 g) unsalted butter
3 3/4 Tbsp (20 g) cocoa powder
3/4 C (150 g) sugar
2 eggs
A ⌐ 1/2 C (50 g) cake flour
    | 1/2 tsp baking powder
    └ Dash salt
1 oz (30 g) walnuts

Prep:
Roughly chop butter. Roast walnuts in a dry pan, then chop. Whisk eggs. Line pan with baking paper. Preheat oven to 320°F (160°C).

1. Add butter to a heat-safe bowl, cover with plastic wrap and microwave for 2 minutes or until melted. While still hot, add cocoa powder and sugar and whisk thoroughly.
2. Add eggs in phases, whisking thoroughly.
3. Sift in mixture A. Stir with a rubber spatula until flour is completely incorporated. Keep some walnuts for use as decoration, and stir the rest into the batter.
4. Pour batter into pan. Scatter walnuts on top. Bake for 30 minutes at 320°F (160°C). Remove from pan and let cool on a wire rack. Once cooled, slice into thin bricks, wrap individually and place in freezer.

Add dried fruits and cinnamon!
Mini Muffins

Yields a dozen 2" muffins
1/2 C (100 g) each butter, sugar
2/3 C (150 ml) milk
1 1/2 eggs, whisked
A ⌐ 1 1/2 C (180 g) cake flour
    | 2 tsp baking powder
    | 1/2 tsp cinnamon
    └ Dash salt
1 3/4 oz (50 g) each raisins, dried apricots

Prep:
Soak raisins in hot water to reconstitute, then dry well. Roughly chop apricots. Preheat oven to 300°F (150°C).

1. Add butter, sugar and milk to a heat-safe bowl, cover with plastic wrap and microwave for 3 minutes. Stir until butter is completely melted.
2. Add whisked eggs and stir with a rubber spatula.
3. Sift in mixture A and stir until flour is completely incorporated. Stir in raisins and apricots.
4. Pour batter into muffin cups (only fill 70% of the way). Bake at 300°F (150°C) for 30 minutes. They're done when a toothpick can be cleanly inserted. Cool muffins on a wire rack. Wrap each individually and place in freezer.

*These mini desserts can be frozen for up to one month. Let thaw at room temperature.

Cinnamon and cocoa are the secret ingredients!

Azuki and Chestnut Purses

2/3 C (150 g) boiled azuki beans
6 boiled sweet chestnuts
Dash cinnamon
1 tsp cocoa powder

1. Add drained chestnuts to a heat-safe bowl, cover with plastic wrap and microwave for 2 minutes. Smash while still warm.
2. Add azuki beans, cinnamon and cocoa powder and stir. Divide into 20 pieces. Place each in the center of a piece of plastic wrap and twist up to seal, like a purse. Place in freezer.

Just stir and you're done!
The rum gives these a great aroma.

Cream Cheese Balls

3 1/2 oz (100 g) cream cheese
1/2 C raisins
1/4 C walnuts
1 tsp each rum, sugar

Prep:
Bring cream cheese to room temperature. Soak raisins in hot water to reconstitute, then dry well. Roast walnuts in a dry frying pan.

1. Add cream cheese to a bowl and stir with a rubber spatula. Stir in rum and sugar. Stir in raisins and walnuts.
2. Divide into 20 pieces and roll into balls. Wrap each individually and place in freezer.

The rich sesame filling is wonderfully fragrant

Sesame Dumplings

1/3 C (50 g) refined white rice flour
3 Tbsp water
A ⎡ 2 Tbsp black sesame paste
 ⎢ 1 Tbsp sugar
 ⎣ 1/2 tsp sesame oil

1. Add rice flour to a bowl. Slowly add water and stir until the mixture has the stiffness of an earlobe. (Adjust the amount of water as needed.) Roll out into a 1" log and slice into 10 pieces.
2. Combine mixture A to create sesame filling. Flatten a rice dumpling into a circle and place a small amount of sesame filling in the center. Fold up sides of dumpling and shape into a ball. Repeat with remaining dumplings.
3. Bring plenty of water to a boil and add dumplings. Once they rise to the top, they're done. Strain and dry well. Line a baking sheet with baking paper, place dumplings on top and place in freezer. Once frozen, transfer to an air-tight container and freeze.

French Toast Salad Bento

Non-sweet cheesy French toast
is perfect for lunch.
Pair with salad for an
excellent combo.

The texture of
the French toast
contrasts with a
green-filled salad.

Use onion dressing!

French Toast

Serves 1
1 slice bread
Soy Sesame Dressing:
A ⌐ 1 egg
  │ 3 Tbsp parmesan cheese
  │ 1 Tbsp milk
  └ Dash each salt, pepper
Butter, vegetable oil

1. Combine mixture A in a pan. Cut bread into bite-size pieces and soak thoroughly in mixture A.
2. Heat 1 tsp each butter and oil in a frying pan over medium heat. Add toast and cook until browned on both sides.

Green Salad

Serves 1
1 oz (30 g) arugula
3 sprigs watercress
6 cherry tomatoes
Onion Dressing:
  ⌐ 1 Tbsp extra virgin olive oil
  │ 1 tsp white wine vinegar
  │ 1/2 tsp grated onion
  └ Dash each salt, pepper

1. Shred arugula and watercress into bite-size pieces. Remove stems from cherry tomatoes and slice in half.
2. Combine Onion Dressing ingredients.

Arrange:
Add French toast to bento box. Add salad. Pour dressing into a separate container to add to salad before eating.

Parmesan cheese adds richness to the flavor.

Sausage and Baguette Salad Bento

Baste the baguette with butter and toast before combining it with a fresh veggie salad.

Add dill or other herbs for extra punch!

Tartar sauce for dressing!

Veggies and Sausages

Serves 1
1 leaf green lettuce
2 sprigs dill
1 small tomato
3 sausages
Tartar Sauce:
⌐ 1 hard-boiled egg
  1/6 onion, minced
  2 tsp capers
  3 Tbsp mayonnaise
└ Dash each salt, pepper
Vegetable oil, salt

1. Shred lettuce and dill into bite-size pieces. Remove stem from tomato and cut into bite-size wedges. Heat a bit of oil in a frying pan and fry sausages until browned.
2. Make Tartar Sauce: Chop egg. Massage a dash of salt into the onions, rinse and dry. Combine egg and onions with remaining sauce ingredients.

Baguette

Serves 1
4" (10 cm) baguette
Butter, as needed

Quarter baguette lengthwise. Baste with butter and pan-roast or toast.

Arrange:
Add baguette, salad and sausage to bento box. Pour tartar sauce into a separate container and add to salad before eating.

Rinse and drain green vegetables, place in a paper towel-lined container and refrigerate the night before to make them extra crisp. All you need to do in the morning is shred them.

Avocado Bagel Bento

Combine a generous amount of avocado salad with a soft, chewy bagel.

Try tearing the bagel and placing some of the salad on a piece.

Use soy mayo dressing for the avocado salad!

Avocado and Cucumber Salad

Serves 1
1 avocado
2 tsp lemon juice
3 sticks imitation crabmeat
1/4 onion
1/2 small cucumber
A ⎡ 1 Tbsp mayonnaise
  ⎣ 1/2 tsp soy sauce, sesame oil
Salt

1. Slice around avocado pit lengthwise, twist apart halves, remove pit and scoop meat out of the skins. Add avocado meat to a bowl and mash. Add lemon juice.
2. Slice imitation crabmeat in half and pull apart. Thinly slice onions, rub with salt, rinse and dry well. Add crabmeat and onions to avocado and stir. Stir in mixture A.
3. Quarter cucumber lengthwise, remove seeds and dice into 1/4" cubes.

Bagel and Strawberries

Serves 1
1 bagel
Strawberries and butter, to taste

Slice bagel in half and butter. Rinse and dry strawberries.

Arrange:
Spread avocado salad and cucumbers between bagel halves in bento box. Garnish with strawberries.

Adding lemon to the avocado keeps it from oxidizing.

3 Healthy Rice Options

From konjac jelly to wakame seaweed to mutli-grain rice, here's a variety of healthy options taking center stage. They're loaded with fiber and low in calories so you can have a heaping portion. Cook up a large batch and freeze individual portions to make bento-making a cinch.

Shirataki

Multi-Grain

Sprouted Brown Rice

Salsify

Konjac

Wakame

*Wrap individual portions and freeze. When prepping for bentos, microwave until hot. These should keep for about 1 month in the freezer.

The firm, pliant texture of wakame adds another dimension!

Omelet and Wakame Rice Bento

Puffy, soft omelet cooked with baby sardines and the wakame seaweed bring out the rice's simple deliciousness.

 Use seaweed for a healthy boost of minerals.

Wakame Rice

1 1/2 C each rice, water
1 C wakame (salt-cured, reconstituted in water)
1/3 tsp salt

Rinse rice. Add rice and water to rice cooker (or pot) and let soak for 30 minutes. Stir in salt and minced wakame and turn on rice cooker. (If using a pot: Bring water to a boil, lower heat to simmer and cook until water is absorbed.) Once cooked, stir to blend.

Puffy Omelet with Baby Sardines

Serves 1
1 egg
1 Tbsp dried baby sardines (*shirasu*)
1 1/2 Tbsp soup broth (*dashi*)
A ⌈ Pinch salt
    ⌊ 1/3 tsp soy sauce
Vegetable oil

1. Whisk egg in a bowl. Stir in soup broth, sardines and mixture A.
2. Heat 1/2 tsp oil in a frying pan over medium heat. Add egg mixture and scramble.

Arrange:
Add wakame rice to bento box. Top with omelet.

 Adding broth to the egg makes it cook up fluffier.

Spicy Minced Pork and Konjac Rice Bento

Top rice with a veggie-ful pork stir-fry for a hearty meal.

The konjac adds a great toothsome texture!

 Chop the konjac finely so it blends with the rice!

Konjac Rice

1 1/2 C rice, water
1 C finely chopped konjac jelly (about 1/2 block)
1/3 tsp salt

1. Boil konjac briefly then dry roast in a frying pan.
2. Add rice and water to rice cooker (or pot) and let soak for 30 minutes. Stir in salt, lay konjac on top and turn on rice cooker. (If using a pot: Bring water to a boil, lower heat to simmer and cook until water is absorbed.) Once cooked, stir to blend.

Minced Pork and Veggie Stir-Fry

Serves 1
3 oz (80 g) ground pork
1/4 carrot
1/4 onion
5 string beans
1 red chili pepper
1/2 nub ginger
A ⌈ 1 Tbsp each soy sauce,
    ⌊   sugar, sake
Vegetable oil

1. Mince all vegetables and the ginger.
2. Heat 1 tsp oil in a frying pan over medium heat. Stir-fry chili pepper and ginger until fragrant. Add pork and stir-fry until browned.
3. Add vegetables and stir-fry. Add mixture A and stir until the liquid has cooked off.

Arrange:
Add konjac rice to bento box. Add minced pork and veggie stir-fry.

Dry roast the konjac to dehydrate.

Spread konjac evenly over rice before cooking.

Salty miso salmon is a perfect match for multi-grain rice!

Miso Salmon and Multi-Grain Rice Bento

Multi-grain rice is a healthy upgrade from typical bento.

Use a bit more water than normal when cooking the rice!

Multi-Grain Rice

1 1/2 C white rice
1 C multi-grain (or wild) rice
2 1/2 to 2 3/4 C water
1/3 tsp salt

1. Combine both rices and rinse well. Add rice and water to rice cooker (or pot) and let soak for 30 minutes.
2. Stir in salt and turn on rice cooker. (If using a pot: Bring water to a boil, lower heat to simmer and cook until water is absorbed.) Once cooked, stir to blend.

Miso Salmon and Veggies

Serves 1
1 filet raw salmon
1/4 onion
6 snow peas
A ┌ 2 tsp sake
│ 1 tsp each miso, sugar
└ 1/2 tsp soy sauce
Vegetable oil
Seven-spice powder (*shichimi togarashi*)

1. Slice salmon into bite-size pieces on the bias. Slice onions into 1/5" wide wedges. Pull strings off of snow peas and slice in half on the bias. Combine mixture A.
2. Heat 1 tsp oil in a frying pan over medium heat and cook both sides of the salmon. Add onions and gently stir-fry. Add snow peas and mixture A and sauté until the liquid has cooked off.

Arrange:
Add multi-grain rice to bento box. Add miso salmon and veggies.

Mixing the miso and sugar before adding sake and soy sauce makes it easier to blend.

Shrimp Stir-Fry and Sprouted Brown Rice Bento

Sprouted brown rice is nutritious and easy to cook.
Top with a savory stir-fry for a satisfying meal!

The savoriness of the shrimp and pickled *takana* is positively addictive.

Mixed with white rice, the sprouted brown rice is easy to cook!

Sprouted Brown Rice

1 1/2 C white rice
1 C sprouted brown rice
2 1/2 to 2 3/4 C water
1/3 tsp salt

1. Combine rices and rinse. Add rice and water to rice cooker (or pot) and let soak for 30 minutes.
2. Stir in salt and turn on rice cooker. (If using a pot: Bring water to a boil, lower heat to simmer and cook until water is absorbed.) Once cooked, stir to blend.

Shrimp Edamame Stir-Fry

Serves 1
2/3 C (100 g) boiled edamame
1/3 C (50 g) pickled Japanese mustard greens (*takanazuke*)
1 oz (30 g) salad shrimp
Sake, sesame oil, soy sauce

1. Shell edamame. Rinse *takanazuke*, dry well and finely chop.
2. Add *takanazuke* to a frying pan and dry-roast. Add 1 Tbsp sake and stir-fry. Add 1/2 Tbsp sesame oil, stir briefly, and add edamame and shrimp and stir-fry. Once all ingredients are evenly coated with oil, add 1/2 tsp soy sauce and stir-fry.

Arrange:
Add sprouted brown rice to bento box. Add shrimp edamame stir-fry.

Dry-roasting then adding sake to the *takanazuke* helps reduce its strong aroma.

Sesame Chicken and Veggie with Salsify Rice Bento

Match fiber-rich salsify rice with sesame dressed chicken, mushrooms and spinach.

Salsify has a great aroma and hearty texture that's just delicious!

Loaded with shaved salsify!

Salsify Rice

1 1/2 C each rice, water
1 salsify (burdock root/gobo)
1/3 tsp salt

1. Shave salsify into fine chips and soak in water. Drain well.
2. Rinse rice. Add rice and water to rice cooker (or pot) and let soak for 30 minutes. Stir in salt, top with salsify and turn on rice cooker. (If using a pot: Bring water to a boil, lower heat to simmer and cook until water is absorbed.) Once cooked, stir to blend.

Sesame Chicken and Veggies

Serves 1
2 chicken breasts
1/2 pack *shimeji* (pioppini) mushrooms
3 stalks *komatsuna* mustard spinach (or regular spinach)
A ⎰ 2 Tbsp roasted white sesame seeds
⎱ 1/2 Tbsp soy sauce
⎰ 1/2 tsp sugar
Dash ginger juice
Sake, soy sauce

1. Remove tendons and skin from chicken and place in a heat-safe dish. Add 1 tsp sake and a dash of ginger juice, cover with plastic wrap and microwave for 2 minutes or until well done. Let cool still covered.
2. Slice off root ends of mushrooms and break up into small clusters. Wrap in plastic wrap and microwave for 1 minute. Boil spinach then squeeze to drain. Slice into 1 1/2" lengths. Drizzle with 1/2 tsp soy sauce and squeeze to drain once more.
3. Combine mixture A in a bowl. Add chicken shredded into bite-size pieces and veggies and blend.

Arrange:
Add salsify rice to bento box. Top with sesame chicken and veggies.

Just pop the chicken marinated in sake in the microwave for an easy way to cook it.

Pickled plum dressing is super refreshing!

Salad Niçoise and Shirataki Rice Bento

Use fine shirataki noodles for a soft texture.
Chop finely before cooking with the rice.

Shirataki is softer than pure konjac jelly!

Shirataki Rice

1 1/2 C each rice, water
1 C shirataki noodles
1/3 tsp salt

1. Boil shirataki. Drain and slice into 1/2 to 3/4"
lengths. Dry-roast in a frying pan to dehydrate.
2. Rinse rice. Add rice and water to rice cooker
(or pot) and let soak for 30 minutes. Stir in salt,
top with shirataki and turn on rice cooker. (If
using a pot: Bring water to a boil, lower heat to
simmer and cook until water is absorbed.) Once
cooked, stir to blend.

Salad Niçoise with Pickled Plum Dressing

Serves 1
1 small can (3 oz) tuna
1/3 head broccoli
2 soft-boiled quail eggs
A ⌐ 1 Tbsp pickled plum meat
⌐ 1/2 tsp soy sauce
⌐ 1/3 tsp mirin
Soy sauce

1. Drain tuna. Break broccoli into small
bunches, boil and drain.
2. Combine mixture A in a bowl. Add tuna and
broccoli and stir.
3. Peel quail eggs, drizzle with soy sauce and
slice in half.

Arrange:
Add shirataki rice to bento box. Add salad
niçoise and garnish with eggs.

Slice shirataki noodles into
short, bite-size pieces.

Healthy Meat and Seafood Sides

Here are some meat and seafood recipes that balance calories with nutrition.

The mustard gets
your stomach growling.

Pork Rolls with String Beans

Serves 1
3 slices thinly-sliced porkloin
5 string beans
2 tsp wholegrain mustard
Salt, pepper

1. Boil string beans, drain and
let cool. Lay out the pork slices
so one piece slightly overlaps the
next in a vertical line. Dust pork
with salt and brush with mustard.
Place string beans on pork slice
closest to you, then roll up into a
log shape.
2. Place under broiler and broil
until browned, occasionally turn-
ing to ensure thorough cooking.
Dust with salt and pepper. Slice
into bite-size pieces.

Marinate in vinegar to remove
any fishy odors.

Marinated Salmon

Serves 1
1 filet salt-cured salmon (*ama-shio*)
1 1/2" each celery, carrot
A ⌈ 1 Tbsp each white wine
⎮   vinegar, lemon juice
⌊ 1/3 tsp vegetable oil
Pepper

1. Slice salmon into bite-size
pieces, dust with pepper and
broil. Julienne celery and carrot.
2. Lay salmon in a shallow pan
and top with celery and carrot.
Pour in mixture A and marinate
for at least 10 minutes.

Just add a bit of oil to finish!

Chicken and *Zha Cai* Stir-Fry

Serves 1
2 chicken breasts
3/4 oz (20 g) *zha cai* (Szechuan
    vegetable)
Salt, pepper, sake, sesame oil

1. Remove tendons and skin from
chicken breasts and thinly slice.
Dust with salt and pepper and
drizzle with 1 tsp sake.
2. Stir-fry chicken in a non-stick
frying pan over medium heat until
browned. Add *zha cai* and stir-fry
until evenly incorporated. Add a
dash of sesame oil and stir.

Enoki mushrooms add
a crisp texture.

Chicken and Mushroom Meatballs

Boiled and dressed in a chili-like
sauce for a healthy menu option.

Squid in Ketchup Sauce

A dash of chili oil makes for
a spicy dish.

Steamed Swordfish and *Takanazuke*

Serves 1
1 filet swordfish
3/4 oz (20 g) *takanazuke* (pickled
  Japanese mustard greens)
2" leek
1/3 tsp chili oil
Salt, sake

1. Slice swordfish into bite-size
pieces and place in a heat-safe
dish. Dust with 1/3 tsp salt and
drizzle with 1 tsp sake. Finely
chop *takanazuke*. Slice leeks
thinly on the bias. Add both vegetables to the swordfish. Drizzle
with chili oil.
2. Cover swordfish with plastic wrap and microwave for 2
minutes.

Serves 1
1 3/4 oz (50 g) ground chicken
1 small package enoki mushrooms
A ┌ 1/3 whisked egg
     │ 2" leek, minced
     │ Dash each ginger juice, salt
     └ 1/2 tsp potato (or corn) starch
B ┌ 2 tsp soy sauce
     └ 1 tsp each sugar, sake
Vegetable oil

1. Slice off root ends of mushrooms and cut into 3/4" lengths.
Add chicken, mushrooms and
mixture A to a bowl and knead
until sticky.
2. Heat 1/2 tsp oil in a frying pan
over medium heat. Shape chicken
mixture into bite-size meatballs
and place in frying pan. Fry each
side for 3 to 4 minutes or until
lightly browned. Add mixture B,
coating the meatballs.

Serves 1
1 3/4 oz (50 g) squid
1/4 onion
1 Tbsp frozen green peas
A ┌ 1 Tbsp ketchup
     │ 1/2 tsp soy sauce
     └ Dash each sugar, sesame oil
Dash ginger juice
Sake
Potato (or corn) starch

1. Slice squid into bite-size pieces.
Rub with ginger juice, 1 tsp sake
and 1/2 tsp starch.
2. Bring water to a boil in a pot.
Chop onions into bite-size pieces
and add to pot along with green
peas. Drain. Boil squid in the same
water, then drain.
3. Combine mixture A in a heat-
safe dish and microwave for 20
seconds. Stir and dress squid.

Tsukudani Soybeans

Savory Mushroom

Kinpira

Namul-Style Fiddlehead Ferns

Vegetable Sides for Nutritional Balance

4

These vegetable sides can be batch-made in advance and frozen for easy bento preparation. Adding veggies makes the bento colorful and full of vitamins and minerals.

Sweet Fried Tofu

Boiled *Hijiki*

Sweet-and-Salty Beef

*Wrap individual portions and freeze. When prepping for bentos, microwave until hot. These should keep for about 1 month in the freezer.

Rolled Omelet and Boiled *Hijiki* Bento

Yellow omelet and green snow peas make for a colorful feast for the eyes.

Add deep-fried fish cake to the *hijiki* for volume!

Hijiki is rich with iron and fiber!

Boiled *Hijiki*

3/4 oz (20 g) dried *hijiki* scaweed
1/2 carrot
2 deep-fried fish cakes (*satsuma-age*)
A ┌ 1 1/4 C soup broth (*dashi*)
  │ 2 Tbsp sake
  └ 1 Tbsp each sugar, soy sauce

1. Rinse *hijiki* and reconstitute in plenty of water. Drain. Slice carrot into 1" long rectangles. Thinly slice fish cakes.
2. Heat 1/2 Tbsp oil in a pan over medium heat. Add carrots, *hijiki* and fish cake slices (in that order) and stir-fry. Once everything is coated in oil add mixture A. Turn heat to high.
3. Once boiling, return heat to medium and stir until liquid has mostly cooked off.

Rolled Omelet and Snow Peas

Serves 1
1 egg
8 snow peas
A ┌ 1 Tbsp soup broth (*dashi*)
  │ 1 tsp sugar
  │ Pinch salt
  └ 2 to 3 drops soy sauce
Vegetable oil, salt

1. Combine mixture A in a bowl. Whisk in egg.
2. Heat egg skillet over medium heat. Coat with a dash of oil. Pour in half of egg mixture and spread across pan. Once it begins to cook, roll up from the edge to the near side then move to far side of the skillet. Pour in remaining egg mixture. Repeat, rolling in first omelet. Cool, then slice into rounds.
3. Remove strings from snow peas and blanch in lightly salted water. Drain.

Arrange:
Add rice to bento box. Top with boiled *hijiki*, rolled omelet and snow peas.

Stir with a wooden spoon to cook off the liquid.

Grilled Salmon and Kinpira Bento

Cut up some salsify and carrots, fry 'em with sesame and pop it in the freezer for whenever you need it!

A classic Japanese combo that's sure to hit the spot.

Salsify for fiber and carrot for carotene!

Kinpira

Serves 1
1/2 salsify (burdock root/gobo)
1/2 carrot
1 red chili pepper
A ⌐ 1 Tbsp each sugar, sake
  ⌊ 1 Tbsp soy sauce
    2 Tbsp water
Vegetable oil

1. Julienne salsify into 1 3/4" lengths and soak in water. Julienne carrot likewise. Remove stem and seeds from chili pepper.
2. Heat 1/2 Tbsp oil in a frying pan over medium heat. Add chili pepper and stir-fry until fragrant. Dry salsify thoroughly and add to frying pan. Stir-fry for 4 to 5 minutes or until tender.
3. Add carrots and stir. Add mixture A and stir until liquid has cooked off.

Grilled Salt-Cured Salmon and Broccoli

Serves 1
1 filet salt-cured salmon (*ama-shio*)
3 florets broccoli
Sake, salt

1. Drizzle salmon with 1 tsp sake and place under broiler and broil for 4 to 5 minutes.
2. Blanch broccoli in lightly salted water. Drain.

Arrange:
Add rice to bento box and top with a sheet of roasted nori seaweed. Add kinpira, salmon and broccoli.

Use a mandoline to make julienning veggies a snap!

Beef, Asparagus and Namul-Style Fiddlehead Ferns Bento

Add *gochujang* (Korean chili paste) for a dash of Korean spice in your bento. Combine with grilled beef and boiled asparagus.

> Sweet-'n-spicy, Korean-style. This recipe will make that rice disappear in no time.

Ferns are packed with fiber.
Use boiled versions to make prep a snap!

Namul-Style Fiddlehead Ferns

7 oz (200 g) boiled fiddlehead ferns
1 Tbsp roasted white sesame seeds
A ┌ 1 Tbsp soy sauce
  │ 1 tsp each *gochujang*, sugar
  │ Grated garlic, to taste
  └ 1/2 C water
Sesame oil

1. Blanch ferns and chop into bite-size pieces.
2. Heat 1/2 Tbsp sesame oil in a frying pan over medium heat. Add ferns and stir-fry. Add mixture A and simmer over low heat for 3 to 4 minutes. Add sesame seeds once liquid has mostly cooked off.

Grilled Beef and Boiled Asparagus

Serves 1
3 oz (80 g) beef tenderloin, thinly sliced
2 asparagus
A ┌ 1 Tbsp minced leek
  │ 2 tsp soy sauce
  │ 1 tsp roasted white sesame seeds
  │ 1 tsp each mirin, sesame oil
  └ Dash pepper
Salt

1. Slice beef into bite-size pieces and massage with mixture A. Heat a non-stick frying pan over medium heat. Spread beef along frying pan and cook both sides until browned.
2. Peel tough root ends of asparagus and slice into small pieces on the bias. Boil in lightly salted water. Drain.

Arrange:
Add rice to bento box. Add ferns, beef and asparagus.

Cooking the moisture out of the ferns before adding seasonings makes them easier to flavor.

Stock Veggie Sides

These vegetable sides are valuable because you can make them in batches in advance and just pop into a bento. Add one of these sides for a dash of color or as a quick palate cleanser.

Sweet and sour for a winning dish
Fried Cucumber Pickles

2 small cucumbers
1 red chili pepper
1/2 nub ginger
A ⌐ 1 1/2 Tbsp each vinegar,
   ⎸   sugar
   ⎸ 2 tsp soy sauce
   └ 1/4 tsp salt
Vegetable oil

1. Roughly chop cucumbers. Remove stem and seeds from chili pepper. Julienne ginger.
2. Add 1 tsp oil and chili pepper to a frying pan and heat over medium heat. Once fragrant, add cucumbers and ginger and stir-fry. Once everything is coated in oil, add mixture A and stir briefly. Pour into storage container.

Just a touch of spiciness
Sweet-and-Sour Lotus Root

1 lotus root (*renkon*)
A ⌐ 2 Tbsp each rice vinegar,
   ⎸   soup broth (or water)
   ⎸ 1 Tbsp sugar
   ⎸ 1/2 tsp salt
   └ 1 red chili pepper, minced
Vinegar

1. Quarter lotus root lengthwise, then slice into thin wedges. Soak in lightly vinegared water, drain and dry. Combine mixture A in a pot, bring to a boil, then cool.
2. Briefly boil lotus root in water, rinse, then dry. Add lotus root to a storage container, cover with mixture A and marinate for at least 10 minutes.

Just add salted kelp!
Broccoli Raab and Salted Kelp

1 bunch broccoli raab
2 Tbsp (10 g) salted kelp (*shio konbu*)
Salt

1. Blanch broccoli raab, drain and squeeze out moisture. Slice into 1" lengths.
2. Add broccoli raab, kelp and salt to a plastic ziplock bag, press out any air and seal shut. Refrigerate for at least 1 hour.

*Stock veggie sides will keep 2 to 3 days in the refrigerator.

Peppercorns add a lovely aroma

Chinese-Style Pickled Daikon and Carrots

A refreshing aftertaste

Ponzu Bell Peppers and Baby Sardines

Try this for Western-style bentos

Honey Pickled Red Onions and Tomatoes

4 small red bell peppers
1 oz (30 g) dried baby sardines
A ┌ 2 Tbsp ponzu soy sauce
  │ 1 Tbsp water
  │ 1/3 tsp soy sauce
  └ 1/4 tsp salt

1. Remove stem and seeds from bell peppers and chop into thin strips. Blanch, then drain.
2. Combine mixture A in a storage container. Stir in baby sardines and bell peppers. Can be eaten right away.

3" (8 cm) daikon radish
1/2 carrot
A ┌ 3 Tbsp vinegar
  │ 1 Tbsp sugar
  │ 1/2 Tbsp soy sauce
  │ 1 red chili pepper
  └ 1/2 nub ginger, thinly sliced
1 tsp whole peppercorns
  (preferably Szechuan)
Salt, vegetable oil, sesame oil

1. Slice daikon and carrot into 1 1/2" rectangular strips. Dust with 1 tsp salt and let sit until tender. Thoroughly squeeze out moisture.
2. Combine mixture A in a storage container. Add vegetables and stir.
3. Heat 1 tsp each vegetable and sesame oils in a frying pan. Add peppercorns and stir. Pour into storage container and let sit for at least 30 minutes.

1 red onion
12 cherry tomatoes
A ┌ 3 Tbsp white wine vinegar
  │ 1 1/2 Tbsp honey
  │ 1 Tbsp each white wine, water
  │ 1/2 tsp salt
  └ 1 bay leaf

1. Chop red onion into bite-size wedges. Remove stems from tomatoes. Combine mixture A in a pot and bring to a boil, then cool.
2. Add onions and tomatoes to a storage container and pour cooled mixture A on top. Marinate for at least 30 minutes.

Ham Cutlet and Savory Mushroom Bento

This recipe uses three different mushrooms, each with their own flavors and textures. Pair with easy ham cutlets and bell peppers with *yukari* seasoning.

Salty, savory boiled mushrooms go so well with rice.

Mushrooms are low in calories and high in fiber.

Savory Mushroom

1 pack shimeji mushrooms
1 small bag enoki mushrooms
4 fresh shiitake mushrooms
1/3 oz (10 g) bonito (*katsuo*)
   flakes
A ⎡ 2 Tbsp sake
  ⎜ 1 1/3 Tbsp soy sauce
  ⎣ 1/2 Tbsp mirin

1. Slice root ends off of shimeji
and break into small clusters.
Slice root ends off of enoki, slice
in half widthwise and break into
small clusters. Remove roots
from shiitake and thinly slice.
2. Add mushrooms and mixture A
to a frying pan and simmer over
medium heat, stirring occasionally, for 5 to 6 minutes or until
liquid is cooked off. Remove from
heat, add bonito flakes and stir.

Ham Cutlets

Serves 1
4 slices roasted ham
Flour, whisked egg, panko bread-
   crumbs, as needed
Pepper
Oil for frying

1. Layer all four ham slices on
top of each other. Dust with pepper and slice in half. Dust with
flour, baste with egg and coat
with breadcrumbs (in that order).
2. Heat frying oil in a frying pan.
Add cutlets and fry both sides
until crispy. Remove and drain oil.

Bell Pepper with *Yukari*

Serves 1
1 green bell pepper
Dash yukari (dried plum rice
   seasoning)

1. Remove stem and seeds from
bell pepper and julienne widthwise. Blanch, then drain.
2. Stir in yukari seasoning.

Arrange:
Add rice to bento box. Top with
mushrooms, ham cutlets and
seasoned bell peppers.

Mushrooms shrink when
cooked, so be sure to use
plenty.

69

Sweet Fried Tofu Bento

Boil up some deep-fried tofu in a sweetened broth, slice and add to your bento. It's much faster than making *inari* sushi, where the rice is stuffed inside the fried tofu.

> The flavor is just like *inari* sushi!

Thin fried tofu is full of protein and calcium.

Sweet Fried Tofu

4 sheets thin fried tofu (*abura-age*)
1 C soup broth (*dashi*)
Sugar, soy sauce

1. Boil tofu to wick away oil. Drain. Slice into bite-size strips. Add tofu to pan with broth and boil for 3 to 4 minutes.
2. Add 1 1/2 Tbsp sugar and boil for an additional 2 to 3 minutes. Add 1 Tbsp soy sauce. Place parchment paper on top of tofu, turn heat to low and boil until most of the liquid has cooked off.

String Beans and Baby Sardines

Serves 1
5 string beans
1 Tbsp dried baby sardines (*chirimen jako*)
Sake, soy sauce, sesame oil, salt

1. Slice string beans into 1 1/2" lengths. Heat 1 tsp sesame oil in a frying pan and sauté string beans over medium heat.
2. Once beans are coated with oil, add 1 tsp sake, baby sardines, 1/4 tsp soy sauce and a dash of salt and stir-fry.

Arrange:
Add rice to bento box. Top with tofu and string beans with baby sardines. Garnish with cherry tomatoes.

Covering with paper while boiling ensures that every part will be evenly seasoned.

Tsukudani Soybeans, Spinach and Egg Bento

Richly flavored soybeans, fresh spinach and boiled eggs—a simple, delicious bento.

Boiled soybeans have a great toothsome texture!

Soybeans are packed with nutrients, including protein, vitamin B1 and vitamin B2!

Tsukudani Soybeans

5 oz (140 g) boiled soybeans
1 oz (30 g) dried baby sardines (*chirimen jako*)
1/2 onion
A ⌐ 1 Tbsp each mirin, sake, soy sauce
  └ 1 tsp miso
Sesame oil

1. Thinly slice onion along the grain.
2. Heat 1/2 Tbsp sesame oil in a frying pan over medium heat. Add onions and sauté until tender. Add soybeans, baby sardines and mixture A and stir. Turn heat to low and simmer, stirring until liquid has mostly cooked off.

Spinach with Nori and Boiled Egg

Serves 1
4 small bunches spinach
2 sheets seasoned nori seaweed
1 boiled egg
Roasted black sesame seeds, as needed
Soy sauce

1. Boil spinach, then drain. Squeeze out excess moisture and chop into 1 1/2" lengths. Drizzle with 1 light tsp soy sauce, stir, and squeeze out excess moisture. Shred nori into small pieces and mix into spinach.
2. Peel boiled egg and slice in half. Sprinkle with black sesame seeds.

Arrange:
Add rice to bento box. Add *tsukudani* soybeans, spinach and boiled egg.

Miso paste adds richness to the flavor.

Sweet-and-Salty Beef and Konjac Bento

Pair light, crisp *komatsuna* with this rich, dense beef recipe.

Salty-sweet beef goes great with white rice. Add pickled ginger for a wonderful flavor balance!

Using konjac subtracts calories!

Sweet-and-Salty Beef

7 oz (200 g) thinly sliced beef
5 oz (150 g) konjac, thinly sliced
1 nub ginger
A ┌ 2 Tbsp each sake, water
  │ 1 1/2 Tbsp sugar
  └ 1 tsp vinegar
B ┌ 2 Tbsp soy sauce
  └ 1/2 Tbsp each mirin, honey
Vegetable oil

1. Slice beef into bite-size pieces and drizzle with 2 tsp oil. Thinly slice ginger. Blanch konjac, slice into bite-size lengths and add to frying pan and dry roast.
2. Add ginger and mixture A to a pan and bring to a boil. Add beef and stir for 2 to 3 minutes. Remove beef.
3. Add mixture B to pan, bring to a boil, and add beef. Add konjac and stir to coat.

Sesame *Komatsuna*

Serves 1
4 stalks *komatsuna* mustard spinach (or regular spinach)
A ┌ 1 tsp sesame oil
  └ 2 pinches salt
Dash roasted white sesame seeds

Boil *komatsuna*, drain and chop into 1 1/2" pieces. Squeeze out any excess moisture. Stir in mixture A and sprinkle with sesame seeds.

Arrange:
Add rice to bento box. Top with beef, konjac and *komatsuna* and garnish with pickled ginger slices.

Dry-roasting the konjac allows the seasoning to seep in more thoroughly.

For Delicious Bento...

1 Choose good containers for bentos.

You don't need special bento boxes for these bento recipes.
All you need is something with a tightly-fitting lid. Use any material
or shape you like, whether it's plastic, enamel, metal or wood.

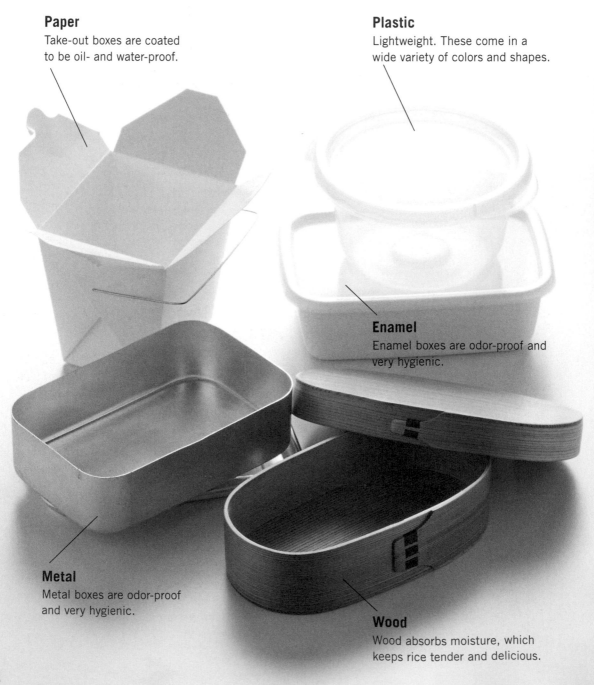

Paper
Take-out boxes are coated
to be oil- and water-proof.

Plastic
Lightweight. These come in a
wide variety of colors and shapes.

Enamel
Enamel boxes are odor-proof and
very hygienic.

Metal
Metal boxes are odor-proof
and very hygienic.

Wood
Wood absorbs moisture, which
keeps rice tender and delicious.

2 Cool the rice and toppings in separate dishes.

Let the rice and toppings cool thoroughly before packing together in the bento box. Packing everything in the bento box while still hot causes condensation and can cause food to spoil quickly.

3 Make sure sauces are well absorbed.

Make sure the sauces used for the toppings are well-absorbed or solidified or the rice will get too soggy or the bento box leak. Either drain off excess liquid or add sesame seeds or bonito flakes to soak up extra sauce.

4 Use small kitchen tools.

Since bentos serve just one, use small boards, knives and frying pans. This makes taking out, cleaning and putting away tools very easy for efficient bento making.

5 Keep batches of stock veggie sides and rice handy.

Making big batches of toppings and sides makes putting bentos together a snap. With kinpira, boiled *hijiki*, etc., wrap individual servings separately and freeze. You can also freeze batches of the healthy rice options in chapter 3 to make things more convenient.

*You can freeze all the recipes from pages 42 to 55 (healthy rice options) and pages 58 to 75 (vegetable sides).

6 Use freezable desserts!

Frozen desserts can be taken from home still frozen. They'll be perfectly thawed by lunch time. Try muffins, brownies or rice dumplings for a Japanese twist.

*See pages 34 to 35 for freezable desserts.

Reference Guide

Common Ingredients in Japanese Cooking

Mirin (sweet, seasoned rice wine)
Can be found in finer grocery stores and Asian markets.
Substitutions
1 tbsp dry sherry + 1/2 tsp sugar.
Or, use sweet sherry.
Or, heat two parts sake and one part sugar.

Thin Fried Tofu (*aburaage*)
Aburaage is a thin sheet of fried tofu. It can be stuffed with rice to make Inari sushi.

Miso (soybean paste)
Can be found in finer grocery stores and Asian markets.

Sake (rice wine)
Substitutions: white wine, white cooking wine

Baby Sardines
A common ingredient used to flavor rice or vegetables. Raw baby sardines are *shirasu*; sardines that have been boiled and dried are *chirimen jako*.
Can be found in Asian markets.

Common Components

Roasted Sesame Seeds
Place sesame seeds in a single layer on a sheet pan and roast in a 350° oven for about 10 minutes. Cool and store in an airtight container.

Mentsuyu (Noodle sauce)
1/2 C water
1 Tbsp each soy sauce, sugar and mirin

Combine everything in a pot and simmer until sugar has melted. Cool before use.

Tsukudani Kelp
1 oz kelp (*konbu*)
1 Tbsp sake
1 tsp rice vinegar
1 Tbsp sugar
1 Tbsp soy sauce

Slice kelp into thin strips. Add kelp, sake and vinegar to a pan. Add just enough water to cover kelp. Bring to a boil then lower heat and simmer kelp until tender. Add soy sauce and sugar. Simmer until liquid has cooked off.

Online Resources

To buy ingredients

www.asianfoodgrocer.com
www.koamart.com
www.savoryspiceshop.com
www.japansuper.com
www.sushifoods.com

For information on ingredients and substitutions

www.foodsubs.com
(aka The Cook's Thesaurus)
www.gourmetsleuth.com
www.asiafood.org

Ten-Minute Bento
by Megumi Fujii

Art Direction and Design: Yoshiro Nakamura + Yen
Stylist: Kayo Sakagami
Photography: Shigeki Aoto (Kodansha Photography Department)

Translation: Maya Rosewood
Vetting: Maria Hostage

Fujii Megumi No Asa, 10 pun De Nokke Bento
© 2007 Megumi Fujii. All rights reserved.
First published in Japan in 2007 by Kodansha Ltd., Tokyo.
This English edition rights arranged through Kodansha Ltd.

Published by Vertical, Inc., New York

ISBN: 978-1-935654-41-4

Manufactured in the United States of America

First Edition

Fifth Printing

Vertical, Inc.
451 Park Avenue South
7th Floor
New York, NY 10016
www.vertical-inc.com